D1517547

A Robbie Reader

EZEKIEL ELLIOTT

Joanne Mattern

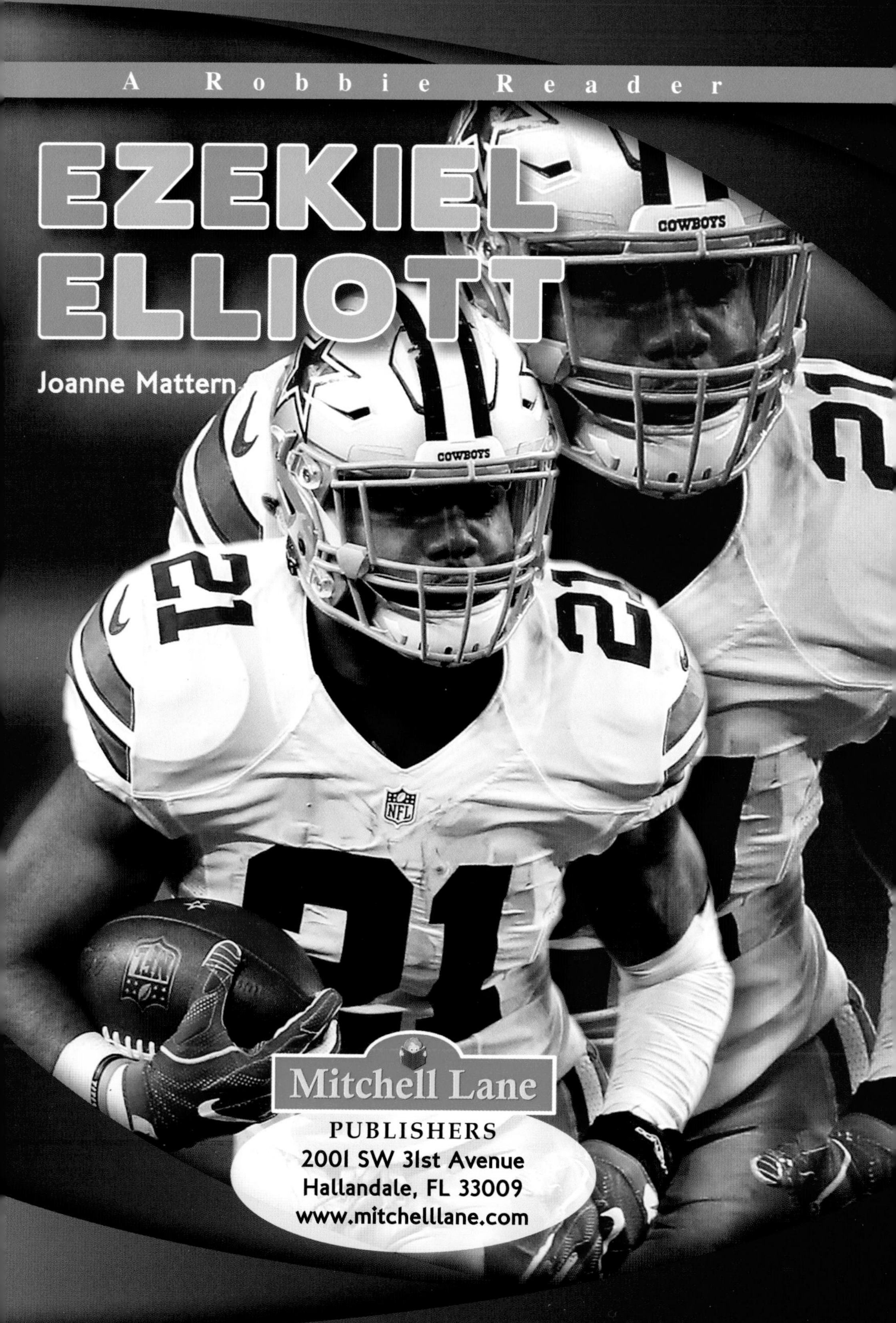

Mitchell Lane
PUBLISHERS
2001 SW 31st Avenue
Hallandale, FL 33009
www.mitchelllane.com

Printing   1   2   3   4   5   6   7   8   9

A Robbie Reader Biography

Aaron Rodgers
Abigail Breslin
Adam Levine
Adrian Peterson
Albert Einstein
Albert Pujols
Aly and AJ
Andrew Luck
AnnaSophia Robb
Ariana Grande
Ashley Tisdale
Brenda Song
Brittany Murphy
Bruno Mars
Buster Posey
Carmelo Anthony
Charles Schulz
Chris Johnson
Clayton Kershaw
Cliff Lee
Colin Kaepernick
Dak Prescott
Dale Earnhardt Jr.
Darius Rucker
David Archuleta

Debby Ryan
Demi Lovato
Derrick Rose
Donovan McNabb
Drake Bell & Josh Peck
Dr. Seuss
Dustin Pedroia
Dwayne Johnson
Dwyane Wade
Dylan & Cole Sprouse
Ed Sheeran
Emily Osment
Ezekiel Elliott
Hailee Steinfeld
Hilary Duff
Jamie Lynn Spears
Jennette McCurdy
Jeremy Lin
Jesse McCartney
Jimmie Johnson
Joe Flacco
Johnny Gruelle
Jonas Brothers
Keke Palmer
Larry Fitzgerald

LeBron James
Mia Hamm
Michael Strahan
Miguel Cabrera
Miley Cyrus
Miranda Cosgrove
Philo Farnsworth
Raven-Symoné
Rixton
Robert Griffin III
Roy Halladay
Shaquille O'Neal
Story of Harley-Davidson
Sue Bird
Syd Hoff
Tiki Barber
Tim Howard
Tim Lincecum
Tom Brady
Tony Hawk
Troy Polamalu
Tyler Perry
Victor Cruz
Victoria Justice

Library of Congress Cataloging-in-Publication Data
Names: Mattern, Joanne, 1963–
Title: Ezekiel Elliott / by Joanne Mattern.
Description: Hallandale, FL : Mitchell Lane Publisher, [2018] | Includes index.
Identifiers: LCCN 2017026940 | ISBN 9781680201208 (library bound)
Subjects: LCSH: Elliott, Ezekiel, 1995– —Juvenile literature. | Football players—United States—
   Biography—Juvenile literature.
Classification: LCC GV939.E46 M37 2018 | DDC 796.332092 [B] —dc23
LC record available at https://lccn.loc.gov/2017026940

eBook ISBN: 978-1-68020-121-5

ABOUT THE AUTHOR: Joanne Mattern is the author of many books for children on a variety of subjects, including history and biography. She has written many biographies for Mitchell Lane. Joanne loves to learn about people, places, and events and bring historical figures to life for today's readers. She lives in New York State with her husband, children, and several pets.

PUBLISHER'S NOTE: The following story has been thoroughly researched and to the best of our knowledge represents a true story. While every possible effort has been made to ensure accuracy, the publisher will not assume liability for damages caused by inaccuracies in the data, and makes no warranty on the accuracy of the information contained herein. This story has not been authorized or endorsed by Ezekiel Elliott.

TABLE OF CONTENTS

Chapter One
A Chip on His Shoulder 5

Chapter Two
A Multi-Sport Star... 9

Chapter Three
College Champion 13

Chapter Four
Rookie Sensation 17

Chapter Five
A Bright Future...23

Statistics 26
Chronology 27
Find Out More...28
    Books...28
    On the Internet 28
    Works Consulted 28
Glossary 31
Index...32

Words in **bold** type can be found in the glossary.

Ezekiel Elliott tries to reach the end zone during the Missouri state high school football championships in 2011. His team, the Bombers, lost the game. Ezekiel was unhappy that he was never able to lead his school to a state championship.

A Chip on His Shoulder

Ezekiel Elliott had a spectacular career as a high school football running back in Missouri. He was good enough to play in the 2013 U.S. Army All-American Bowl. Ezekiel was a speedster who won four events in the state high school track championships as a senior. But one thing frustrated him. In his junior and senior years, his football team played for the state championship. Both times they lost in the final moments. And his track team finished second despite Ezekiel's outstanding effort. So as he told *Sports Illustrated for Kids*, "That was a chip I had on my shoulder. I had never won a team championship."

Ezekiel thought he could get rid of that chip by attending Ohio State University.

The Buckeyes were consistently one of the country's best football programs. Ezekiel didn't play much as a **freshman**. But as a **sophomore**, he was the team's leading rusher as Ohio State won 12 games and lost only one in the regular season.

The Buckeyes played the Oregon Ducks for the national championship on January 12, 2015. Ezekiel saved his best for last. He rushed for 246 yards and scored four touchdowns. The Buckeyes defeated the Ducks 42–20. Ezekiel was named the game's Offensive MVP (most valuable player).

"The way Elliott racked up his yardage was the most impressive part," wrote Nicole Auerbach of *USA Today*. "He bulldozed the Oregon defense; that's the only way to put it. The Ducks knew he'd get the ball, and he'd run it up the middle–effectively– anyway. He averaged nearly 7 yards a carry."

"When you have a back who runs like that, it's easy to block for him," added Buckeye offensive tackle Taylor Decker.

Ezekiel's championship dreams finally came true in 2015 when he helped his college football team, the Ohio State Buckeyes, win the national championship. Here Ezekiel poses with head coach Urban Meyer and the championship trophy.

"He doesn't back down from a defensive lineman. He's 180 miles per hour all the time."

As Ezekiel joined his **jubilant** teammates after the game, he was just a little bit lighter. The chip on his shoulder was gone.

Ezekiel Elliott carries the ball into the end zone during the Missouri state high school football championships in 2012. Despite Ezekiel's hard work, his team lost the game.

A Multi-Sport Star

Ezekiel Elliott was born on July 22, 1995, in St. Louis, Missouri. His parents, Stacy and Dawn Elliott, had been star athletes at the University of Missouri. Dawn ran track. Stacy played linebacker on the football team. Ezekiel has two younger sisters, Aaliyah and Lailah. They are great athletes too.

Ezekiel's parents knew that education was very important. Stacy told 5pointsblue. com, "Dawn and I sacrificed to provide a high-quality education for Ezekiel and his sisters. We didn't drive the best cars. We didn't go on fine trips or live in big houses. . . . Our family vacations were AAU national track championships held in places across the country."

His parents' sacrifices let Ezekiel attend John Burroughs School. It is a **private school** in a suburb of St. Louis. The school has a strong reputation for preparing its students to get into the best colleges. Ezekiel did well in school, and he really excelled at sports. He was a superstar on the track team. He was named the Gatorade Track Athlete of the Year in Missouri.

Ezekiel really loved playing football. When he joined the John Burroughs football team, Coach Gus Frerotte told him to be a team **role model**. "If he complained about running, everyone else would complain about running," Frerotte told *Sports Illustrated for Kids*. "But if he shut up and ran, everyone else would shut up and run too."

As a **junior** in 2012, Ezekiel rushed for 1,802 yards and 45 touchdowns. He also caught 23 passes for 401 yards and six scores. Ezekiel's stats were even better during his **senior** year. He had 3,061 total yards and 50 touchdowns. He was listed as the country's ninth-best high school running back.

Many people thought Ezekiel would follow in his parents' footsteps to the University of Missouri. However, Ezekiel chose Ohio State instead. "I felt like no fan base could rival Ohio State," Ezekiel told *Sports Illustrated for Kids*. "There was an energy that I just didn't feel anywhere else in the country."

Ezekiel (#15) jumps to avoid a tackle during a game between his Ohio State Buckeyes and the San Diego State Aztecs in 2013. Ohio State won big, 42-7.

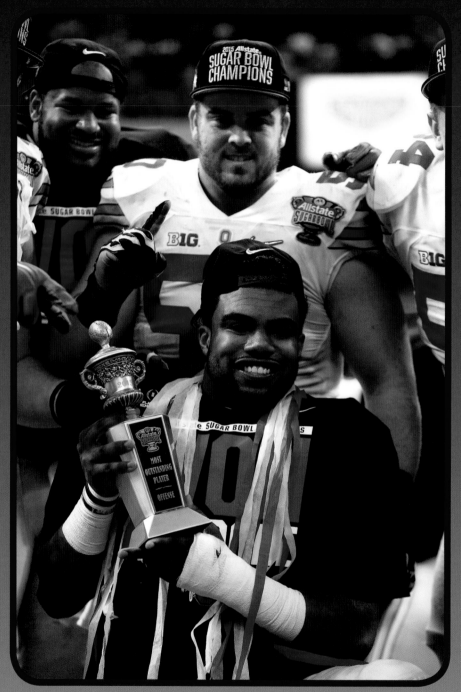

Ezekiel is all smiles as he and his teammates celebrate their win over the Alabama Crimson Tide during the Allstate Sugar Bowl on January 1, 2015. Eleven days later they beat the Oregon Ducks to become national champions.

College Champion

Ezekiel went to Ohio State full of confidence. However, he did not see much playing time during his freshman year. The Buckeyes had a great running back named Carlos Hyde. Then, in 2014, Ezekiel got his chance to start. He ran for 1,878 yards and 18 touchdowns. His rushing total was the second-highest in Ohio State history. The Buckeyes capped the season by becoming national champions.

His 2015 season was even better than 2014. Before the season started, he told Yahoo! Sports, "I felt like I was a little **underrated** last season, but I don't expect anything to change. I'm still going to try to work harder than anyone on the field and prove myself."

Ezekiel proved himself–and more. He rushed for more than 1,800 yards and scored 23 touchdowns. He was named the Big Ten Offensive Player of the Year and Big Ten Running Back of the Year. Ezekiel became the second-leading rusher in Ohio State's history, with a total of 3,961 yards. His five 200-yard rushing games are tied for the top spot in school history.

However, Ezekiel's days at Ohio State were coming to an end. He announced that he was leaving school to enter the 2016 National Football League (NFL) **draft**. Ezekiel was confident he could handle the pressure of playing in the NFL. "I can't control where I will play, so I'll just grind and give maximum effort every practice and every game and work hard and be consistent," he explained to sbnation.com. "And just keep dreaming. And remind myself every day of all I did and all it took to get there."

The Dallas Cowboys made Ezekiel the fourth overall pick in the draft. The team's executive vice president, Stephen Jones, told ESPN that a lot was riding on him. "When

Ezekiel wears an unusual outfit as he poses proudly with his parents at the NFL draft in April 2016.

you take a player that high in the draft, you have really high expectations. We've got good running backs on this team, but we really just felt like he could bring something very special to the table."

Ezekiel poses with NFL Commissioner Roger Goodell and his new jersey after the Dallas Cowboys made Ezekiel the fourth overall selection in the 2016 draft.

CHAPTER FOUR

Rookie Sensation

Ezekiel signed a four-year rookie contract with the Cowboys. The contract was for $24.9 million with a $16.3 million signing bonus. Ezekiel was in the big leagues now, and he meant to be the best.

Ezekiel quickly justified the team's faith in him. He became only the third running back in NFL history to rush for 1,000 yards after just the ninth game of his first season in the league. Two weeks later, he **surpassed** Cowboys legend Tony Dorsett's team rookie rushing record.

Scoring touchdowns made Ezekiel happy. In a game against the Tampa Bay Buccaneers on December 18, 2016, Ezekiel ran into the end zone and jumped into a

Ezekiel Elliott pushes away a tackler as he carries the ball in a game against the Washington Redskins in November 2016.

giant Salvation Army kettle. It was there to remind fans that the organization's holiday charity drive was collecting donations to buy gifts for poor families.

The NFL threatened to fine Ezekiel. He promised to donate the amount of his fine to the Salvation Army. The league backed down, but Ezekiel donated $21,000 to the charity anyway. He tweeted a reminder to fans that "Your $21 feeds a family for three days." The Salvation Army benefited even more from Ezekiel's kettle leap. Within 12 hours, it received $182,000 in online donations.

Ezekiel finished the season as the NFL's top rusher with 1,631 yards. He led the league with 322 carries and placed third with 15 touchdowns. "He certainly handled the opportunities we gave him really well, both as a runner, blocker, and as a receiver," Cowboys coach Jason Garrett told the Fort Worth *Star-Telegram*.

Ezekiel was selected as a First-Team All-Pro and was chosen to play in the Pro Bowl. His rookie teammate, quarterback

After scoring a touchdown against the Tampa Bay Buccaneers in December 2016, Ezekiel was so excited that he jumped into a Salvation Army kettle in the end zone. Ezekiel's stunt led to a huge increase in donations to the Army.

Ezekiel and his close friend and teammate Dak Prescott (#4) enjoy a quiet moment as they watch their team during a practice for the 2017 Pro Bowl.

Dak Prescott, was also chosen for the Pro Bowl. Ezekiel and Dak were the first rookie running back and quarterback teammates in NFL history to be selected for the game in the same year.

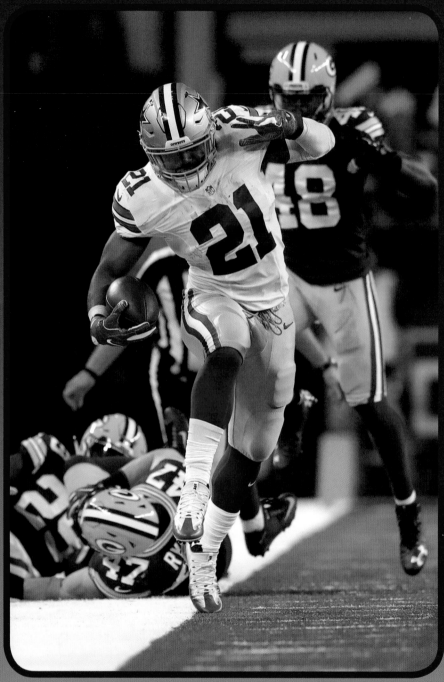

Ezekiel carries the ball during the fourth quarter against the Green Bay Packers in the NFC divisional playoff game in January 2017. The Packers would go on to win the game.

CHAPTER FIVE

A Bright Future

Now it was off to the **playoffs** for
Ezekiel and the Cowboys. But Dallas lost
to the Green Bay Packers. However, Ezekiel
rushed for 125 yards. That made him just
the second Cowboys rookie to rush for over
100 yards in a playoff game. Ezekiel's first
NFL season was done, and it **confirmed**
what everyone said: He is one of the best
players in the game.

Ezekiel also makes sure to use his
celebrity to help others. Like his Cowboys
teammates, he does a lot of charity work.
He also works to raise awareness of people
and even animals in need.

In December 2016, NFL players wore
cleats with a picture that showed support

for a cause. Ezekiel chose a picture of his dog, Ace, to campaign against animal cruelty and encourage people to adopt from animal shelters. Ezekiel also sponsored an "Adopt a Pet" day at a local shelter.

Ezekiel reaches out to human fans too. In 2016, a Massachusetts teenager named Halle Silver sent an Instagram message to several current and former players at Ohio State. She asked them to do something to cheer up her brother, Jake, as he underwent treatment for cancer. Halle also displayed orange wristbands printed with the words "Silver Strong." The family was selling them to raise money for Jake's treatments.

Halle was stunned when Ezekiel sent her a message. "I want one of those bands," he told her. "Send me a bunch. I'll wear it all season." Ezekiel kept his promise, wearing the orange bracelet in every game of the season. He also sent many messages to Halle and Jake as the teenager's treatment went on. "It's inspirational for [Jake] to see me out there having the year I am, wow, wearing something that's personal

Ezekiel loves his fans and will happily go out of his way to meet them and pose for photos.

and close to him. I feel like we kind of have a connection there," he told dallasnews.com.

As his career continues, Ezekiel Elliott will **strive** to be the best player and role model he can be, both on and off the field.

RUSHING STATISTICS

SEASON	TEAM	GP	ATT	YDS	AVG	LNG	TD	FD	FUM	LST
2016	DALLAS	15	322	1,631	5.1	60	15	91	5	1
Career		15	322	1,631	5.1	60	15	91	5	1

RECEIVING STATISTICS

SEASON	TEAM	GP	REC	TGTS	YDS	AVG	LNG	TD	FD	FUM	LST
2016	DALLAS	15	32	40	363	11.3	83	1	11	0	0
Career		15	32	40	363	11.3	83	1	11	0	0

GP=Games played; ATT=Pass attempts; REC=Total receptions; TGTS=Receiving Targets; YDS=Passing yards; AVG=Yards per pass attempt; LNG=Longest pass play; TD=Passing touchdowns; FD=First downs; FUM=Total fumbles; LST=Fumbles lost

CHRONOLOGY

1995	Ezekiel Elliott is born in St. Louis, Missouri, on July 22.
2009–2013	Ezekiel is a star athlete at John Burroughs School in Missouri.
2013	Ezekiel begins his Ohio State football career.
2014	Ezekiel becomes the starting running back for the Buckeyes.
2015	Ezekiel leads the Buckeyes to the national championship.
2016	Ezekiel is chosen by the Dallas Cowboys as the fourth overall pick in the NFL draft; he becomes the starting running back for the Cowboys and leads the league in rushing.
2017	Ezekiel is named to the NFL All-Pro First Team and to the Pro Bowl.

FIND OUT MORE

Books

Glave, Tom. *Dallas Cowboys*. Minneapolis, MN: Abdo, 2016.

Mack, Larry. *The Dallas Cowboys Story*. Minneapolis, MN: Bellwether Media, 2016.

On the Internet

Ezekiel Elliott: ESPN.com
http://www.espn.com/nfl/player/_/id/3051392/ezekiel-elliott

Ezekiel Elliott: Dallas Cowboys
http://www.dallascowboys.com/team/players/roster/ezekiel-elliott

Ezekiel Elliott Profile: Dallas Cowboys
https://insidethestar.com/dallas-cowboys/players/ezekiel-elliott/0

Works Consulted

Amato, Lauren. "Ezekiel Elliott's Family: The Pictures You Need to See." Heavy.com, April 28, 2016. http://heavy.com/sports/2016/04/ezekiel-elliott-family-dad-stacy-mom-dawn-sisters-instagram-draft-nfl-football-stats-ohio-state-pictures/

Auerbach, Nicole. "Ohio State's Ezekiel Elliott continues his impressive run." *USA Today*, January 13, 2015. https://www.usatoday.com/story/sports/ncaaf/2015/01/13/ezekiel-elliott-ohio-state-college-football-playoff/21676627/

FIND OUT MORE

Boren, Cindy. "Ezekiel Elliott Is Making a Huge Donation to the Salvation Army." *The Washington Post*, December 20, 2016. https://www.washingtonpost.com/news/early-lead/wp/2016/12/20/ezekiel-elliott-is-making-a-huge-donation-to-the-salvation-army/?utm_term=.a4737153756f

———. "Ezekiel Elliott's Subtle Season-Long Gesture to a Young Fan with Cancer." *The Washington Post*, January 14, 2017. https://www.washingtonpost.com/news/early-lead/wp/2017/01/12/ezekiel-elliotts-subtle-season-long-gesture-to-a-young-fan-with-cancer/?utm_term=.445db91c584e

DaSilva, Cameron. "Here's Why Ezekiel Elliott Will Wear Cleats with a Picture of His Dog on Them." Fox Sports, December 9, 2016. http://www.foxsports.com/nfl/story/dallas-cowboys-ezekiel-elliott-custom-cleats-witten-frederick-dog-112916

Epstein, Jori. "Cowboys RB Ezekiel Elliott on wearing cancer patient's bracelet all season: 'He feels like he's there with me.'" https://sportsday.dallasnews.com/dallas-cowboys/cowboys/2017/01/13/cowboys-rb-ezekiel-elliott-wearing-cancer-patient-bracelets-season-feels-like

"Ezekiel Elliott." Gale Biography in Context. October 1, 2016. link.galegroup.com/apps/doc/K1650010459/BIC1?u=nysi_se_sfl&xid=7c41c68f

George, Thomas. "Ezekiel Elliott's Greatness Began in His Mother's Dream." Sbnation.com, April 28, 2016. http://www.sbnation.com/2016/4/28/11526322/ezekiel-elliott-nfl-draft-profile-ohio-state

FIND OUT MORE

Sayles, Damon. "Ezekiel Elliott Never Satisfied." ESPN, June 28, 2012. http://www.espn.com/college-sports-recruiting/football/story/_/id8105304/ohio-state-rb-ezekiel-elliott-never-satisfied

Scales, Kristi. "Ezekiel Elliott Buys His Parents a New House." 5pointsblue.com, May 26, 2016. http://www.5pointsblue.com/ezekiel-elliott-buys-parents-new-house/

Schlabach, Mark. "Elliott, Jones deliver emphatic finish." ESPN, January 13, 2015. http://www.espn.com/college-football/bowls14/story/_/id/12159703/ezekiel-elliott-cardale-jones-propel-ohio-state-buckeyes-college-football-playoff-national-championship

Shute, Lauren. "Ezekiel Elliott, Ohio State's Leading Rusher in 2014, Is Back for More." *Sports Illustrated for Kids*. Aug 13, 2015. https://www.sikids.com/si-kids/2016/01/12/ezekiel-elliott-back-more

Thomas, Jeanna. "Ezekiel Elliott's Salvation Army TD Celebration Led to Huge Spike in Donations." sbnation.com, December 20, 2016. http://www.sbnation.com/2016/12/19/14013046/ezekiel-elliott-salvation-army-td-celebration-donations

GLOSSARY

confirmed (cuhn-FIRMD)–proved

draft (DRAFT)–to select people

freshman (FRESH-muhn)–person in his or her first year in school

jubilant (JOO-buh-luhnt)–very happy

junior (JUNE-yuhr)–person in his or her third year in school

playoffs (PLAY-offs)–games played to decide the championship

private school (PRY-vuht SKOOL)–a school that charges students a fee to attend

role model (ROLL MAH-duhl)–a person who sets a positive example for others to follow

senior (SEEN-yuhr)–person in his or her fourth (and usually final) year in school

sophomore (SAW-fuh-mohr)–person in his or her second year in school

strive (STRYV)–try as hard as possible

surpassed (suhr-PAST)–went beyond

underrated (uhn-der-RAY-tuhd)–not getting full recognition for accomplishments

INDEX

Dallas Cowboys   14–15, 17, 23

Decker, Taylor   6

Dorsett, Tony   17

Elliott, Aaliyah   9

Elliott, Dawn Huff   9

Elliott, Ezekiel
   birth of   9
   family of   9
   at John Burroughs School   10
   chooses Ohio State University   11
   at Ohio State University   13–14
   at NFL draft   14–15
   chosen by Dallas Cowboys   14–15
   2016 season and   17, 19, 21, 23
   kettle leap and   19
   chosen for Pro Bowl   19
   charity work and   23–24, 26

Elliott, Lailah   9

Elliott, Stacy   9

Frerotte, Gus   10

Garrett, Jason   19

John Burroughs School   10

Jones, Stephen   14–15

National Football League (NFL)   14, 17, 19, 21, 23

Ohio State University   5–7, 11, 13–14

Prescott, Dak   21

Pro Bowl   19, 21

Salvation Army   19

Silver, Halle   24

Silver, Jake   24

University of Missouri   9, 11